The Caress of the Rhinoceros

*a collection of poetry by Kate Leigh,
the children of Portsmouth, NH, and beyond*

Copyright © *The Caress of the Rhinoceros*: a collection of poetry by Kate Leigh, the children of Portsmouth, NH, and beyond

All rights reserved.

"Dog" by Hollis Ruby Cannella Matthews, "Spring Snow" by Lulu Higginson, and commentary of both poems by John Simon originally published in EDGE Magazine by Seacoast Media Group.

Credit for photo on pg. 21: S. Flause

Published by Piscataqua Press
an imprint of RiverRun Bookstore
32 Daniel Street
Portsmouth NH 03801

ISBN: 978-1-944393-88-5

*This book is dedicated to Bread and Puppet Theater
for their inspirational commitment to the arts and social change*

Contents

Poems by Kate Leigh — 1

The Story of the Title	1
A Bit of Carbon	3
Apocalypse Poem	4
Back Harbor Bonfire	5
Charged Air	6
Cis-Gender	8
Falling Backwards	10
Flowers Negative	11
Free Time Reverie	12
Grains of Salt	13
How Soon	13
Never Tire	14
Benediction	14
In Garden Muse	15
Notes from Appledore	16
New Day	17
Oceanic Hotel	18
Caress of the Rhinoceros	19
Praises	20
African Burying Ground	22
Rising Waters	23
Shell Game/Puerto Rico	24
Slant View	25
Table of Seasons	27
Seasmoke Lace	28
Weird Intimacy	29
Sangsara	31

Photos — 32-40

Poems for Peace — 41

Foreword	43
I'm Safe – *Judah D'Antonio*	45
Robin – *Eila Fitzgerald*	46
Writer – *Claire Breger-Belsky*	47
Jump – *Mehli Yoder*	48

Terrorists Are Not True Muslims! – *Nuha Al-Shair*	49
Pitter Patter – *Huxley Schintzius*	51
Sleep Softly – *Huxley Schintzius*	51
Two weeks – *Megan Toddy*	52
Dog – *Hollis Ruby Cannella Matthews*	57
Commentary on Dog – *John Simon*	57
Intellectual Regression – *Myla Swallow*	59
Argue with me. – *Myla Swallow*	61
Homemade Candle – *Lulu Higginson*	63
I Believe – *Ella Higginson*	64
Being Female – *Samantha Fitzpatrick*	66
Did You Know the Dalai Lama Sometimes Swats at Mosquitos? – *Mikey Ippolito*	69
Cruising – *Lexi Legendre*	70
Top of Earth – *Lexi Legendre*	71
shame. – *Amelia Sheesley*	72
san fransisco. – *Amelia Sheesley*	73
cxvb. – *Amelia Sheesley*	74
Sway – *Dewey Cora Cannella Matthews*	74
Spring Snow – *Lulu Higginson*	75
Commentary on Spring Snow – *John Simon*	75
Afterword: Kate Leigh, My Mary Poppins – *Wendy Cannella*	77

The Story Of The Title

The Caress Of The Rhinoceros is a line in a poem I wrote on Star Island during the summer of 2017 when the always-inspirational Bread and Puppet Theater performed on the front lawn. It was not a perfect day. The wind was high. Perhaps two dozen performers set up the stage and costume change area behind it. The construction was done with curtains and poles. The set up took most of the morning. All their work was visible to those who wanted to watch. The concentration of the performers upon their tasks was complete.

As a child coming of age in the 60s, I remember Bread and Puppet, always witness to scenes of injustice, always outspoken, always quintessentially artistic, celebrating the creative spirit. Eating meals with them in the communal dining area on Star, I found that "exemplariness" shining through their personalities, communications, sensitivities and actions.

The same is true for people who participate year to year in the working community that runs Star Island each summer season. This group is exceptionally expressive and positive. So there was a symbiosis.

The performance I saw that day, with banners blowing in the stiff gusts off Gosport Harbor, raised my spirits. It put me in mind of my more active and expressive youth, years when I attended peace rallies and marched in my tattered painted jeans in New York and Boston. I daydreamed of my short but significant college days at Antioch in Yellow Springs, and the extraordinary curriculum in the summer of 1969.

My favorite part of anything is Nature. 'Bread' sang and danced for rain forests, costuming as the trees and suffering their falls. They conveyed the extinction of animals in their papier-mâché costumes. They remained humorous while reminding us that our part in the larger ecosystem is often harmful. Bread and Puppet seems to be composed of political activists, actors, artists, musicians, acrobats on stilts, and all age participants.

They employ distraction well, even out of doors on the wide lawn, with no place to hide. As part of the preparations they had positioned a costume near a big rock. It looked like the rock, just a grey heap, until during the show two actors slid into it and waddled down to the stage as a glorious rhinoceros!

That sight twigged my mind to a book of the same name, *Rhinoceros* by Eugene Ianesco. I am happy to say it is still available, as I re-read it when I returned home. To my mind, the book, which is a short play, tells the story of an inward-looking man who is trying to improve himself, partially by confiding his concerns to his friends. They have varying responses, perhaps trying in their own ways to be helpful. Then these characters begin to morph into rhinoceroses. It is an absurd plot with a noticeable nugget of hidden truth.

Now I look out at the world, our country, our struggle to remain in touch with what is good, kind, and aligned with peace. Within ourselves there is our conscience, the part that wants us to evolve. Outside of ourselves we find those qualities where we may, in Bread and Puppet, on Star Island, in our friendships, and within poetry.

So I wrote a poem for Bread and Puppet Theatre. These wonderful performers lived on the island for several days, and were able to attend the weekly "Pel Show" as it is called, a talent show. I was part of the staff that week, so I could participate by reading a poem. "The Caress Of The Rhinoceros."

I want this book to be allowed to make no coherent sense because much of life is absurd. Yet I also want us to caress the inner rhinoceros, the one who forgets things, listens only partially, procrastinates, misses edits, second guesses, and barges through situations. We can evolve, bit by bit. Bread and Puppet and others feed us and light the path. (Literally, they fed us bread they had baked.)

A Bit Of Carbon

A bit of carbon in a tad of fluff
Texts an uber to go to the bus,
Next an airplane, then more public trans
To finally arrive, unpack her stuff.

This little wad of carbon-based brain
Bequeaths the world her small bloodstain,
Four children carry forth if not names
Then the DNA strands in their spiral chains.

Still we simply wake, and
Still the first coffee make.
Still places attract and pull,
Molecules asserting will.

Apocalypse Poem

Night a fearsome stretch,
Lying flat, unable to digest
Bits of cheese and cracker crumbs,
The bittered taste of old wine.

An interruption from
Restless mental rumblings,
The light chain pulled,
Firefly dreams scatter.

So must be the end of times.
Uncertain, rest is sleepless,
A bubble of wishfulness,
Weary one-way tunnel.

Purple mists settle dust.
Beetles curl and roll beneath
Fallen headstones, give up
Until eternity advances.

Darkness complicit with light.
Sad stories range from lack
Of potable water to flooded homes
To a backwash of the ordinary.

Hunkered by rattling windows
The cats stretched tall as
Giraffes, peer at the illusion
That humans trespass within.

Back Harbor Bonfire

Here now the day calls.
Eyes awake to birth of light
From an unscreened window,
The share of open air.

We held a bonfire last night.
Heard stars whisper shape-names.
Sang familiar songs, talked of
Individual plans, boats to take us far,
Schools and schedules.

Crack go wood scraps, snap
The flames, smooth and wrinkled faces both
No better place to be, the fire
Guides us, its dance the emergence of
Bees in a surprise thaw,
The hive free.

Charged Air
Inspired by Celia Thaxter's "Summer Day"

The air is charged with storm particles,
Louder and louder the boom of its voice.
Jags of lightning pierce the distance,
Onward the approach, beyond all choice.

I dip bare feet in the mid-range tide.
The salt and chill serve to conduct
Arousal of the mid-morning mood,
With thunder, then silence, we reflect.

The waters lie in expectant calm
Fiery bolts strike on fluid skin,
The waves gone quiet, whitecaps waned,
No birds or mammals, wing or fin.

Age old changes usher in showers.
A flush of romance, the way ocean
Settles how much time to wait
Until the patter, clamor of motion.

The sea fowl safely follow gusts.
When danger's passed, the soaring refrain
With golden seaweeds that slide, a-stir
In cool effervescence livened by rain.

No hurricane here, just a wet island day,
Just sunlight embanked in clouds of salt mist
That blot sure footholds on formerly known
Townships and skylines, mazes of bliss.

The afternoon wraps us in pearly embrace,
Decades unwound since beholding such sights.
A far shoreline framed in granite's enclave,
Perhaps spirit's home in a past life.

To people who helped preserve these isles
From templates of wasteful, short-sighted abuse,
Praises are due and thanks for protection
From forces other than laudable use.

Abed in the aftermath of a full day,
Blessed by tumult, adorned with some peace,
Words of old poets like swallows surround
As past and present are blended with ease.

Cis-Gender

Those who accept our genital designation,
Who see or feel no ambiguity to our classic
Identifications, though with the universe
Changing in acceleration, adjust to the reality
Of female/male as two ends of a spectrum...

So all we do can be from both inner sexes,
If we need we can change operating parts,
Or simply dress and behave more exactly
How we feel most genuine and authentic, this
And much more, for we now age in place, we
Are fed that sixty is the new thirty, and such.

The world market bends its ways and wares so
Senior citizens care to engage actively.
The rest is resistance to change, to think from
Our usual thinking. But I know a Henry
Who was a Heather, and so do you. When we
Encounter trans-gender, embrace the entire pendulum.

Everything is up for fewer labels, certainly
What we call race is merely color and shape.
Also freedoms such as believer, agnostic, atheist,
Fight for life, opt to die, receiving or leaving treatments...

As we wake up white we dream we are meditating
Fully enlightened, when actually we just stepped on the path,
Start to accept all parts, even ignorance.
So much complexity is introduced by means not intentionally
Insulting, but patiently a reflection of a grander understanding...

Let's think first of the needs of the planet,
As we develop language in place of labels,
Consider our cousins, the animals and plants,
And climb down from the Tower of Babel.

Falling Backwards

All life is falling backwards into the arms
Of someone you hope is behind you.
It is a game of trust and hope and surprises.

But if you tell this secret, no one is listening.
They are busy looking over their shoulders
For the stunt guy who might catch them
(Or possibly pick up the broken pieces
For eventual reassembly).

I have heard that in Japan molten gold
Connects the cracks of smashed vessels
Enhancing their original beauty
With age and authenticity.

I have no extra gold or even silver.
Unless from the sun and the moon
Who, despite my follies, wait on me
Day and night, who are constant and deliver
Genuine light and restful darkness.

What will magnetize my molecules and draw them
Unresisting into the fabric of the universe?
Someday I will fall backwards
Into my own elements.

Flowers Negative

Iris means he sees you know he's got another girl.
Roses say the affair is almost over, I'm coming home.
Gladiolas say you will need them for his funeral
If you ever find out what he did.

Daisies speak a half-hearted attempt
At foreplay, lilies work well for distraction
Due to their strong scent, that covers her perfume.
The dahlias he said he planted himself,
Did his wife weed them, I wonder?

It is not the fault of the flowers, no way.
They are mis-regarded as a peace offering
Or cover-up, for they bring color and joy every day.

A jar of mixed flowers, gathered as they fall
Or need to be thinned. Do not mistakenly
Disrespect flowers, they are no minion of man,
Rather heaven of the earthly realm.

Free Time Reverie

Rocking in a chair by the southwest window
On the third floor of the Grand Hotel,
Overlooking the 'No Swimming' beach
At high tide, a late-blooming sun ray
Highlights glints of isinglass. Seems
A seal slept there 'til morn yesterday.

A solo person seeks refuge in the gazebo,
Where four decades ago I often sat gazing.
The flag is hoisted on Lunging Isle,
There I once hunted waverly whelks, the
Bleached seashells on the sole sandbar,
Submerged at lunar high tides.

I strain to remember how years ago
My path pulled me from this fond Star,
From the Shoals, now playful currents
Wash me so close to my distant past, again
To collect sea treasure from another time,
And nap, a placid seal, with half memories.

Grains Of Salt

Grains of salt abound
In this unchaste ground,
An island cemetery of old.

'Wife of'...'widow of'...

Reasoned insults lessen.
Restore to ancient women
Grains of their truth.

How Soon

How soon the golden apples
Raked in an autumn pile
Soften and collapse to brown.

How soon the fiddley spiders
Find the moist rhododendrons,
Spread thick-spun coverlets.

How soon the fall moon finds
Her way into my bedroom.

Never Tire

I like to live in a place
Where at one hour of the day
I see a full body of water
Shimmering with the reflections
Of each cell of the sun, and
A few hours later, on my return,
Be met by a mud flat,
Its temporary scars show me
The drag and suck of the
Outgoing tide, I never tire of this.

Benediction

To offer small and have it be enough
Only what fits in my palm like a cup
Let it be an egg or seed or a gem
Accept with the heart instead of the hand

In Garden Muse

Bearing the weight of gloomy skies
On my bent back, setting the wilted
Poppy plants cool, with hope of drizzle.
From cast seed these offshoots grew,
Extra bowed green bodies passed to me.
I sink them in corners gratefully, for poppies
Of all hues, in their sublime fragility
Tell of Celia's own generative ability.

Her floral haven of inclusive design, where
Each flower reigns recognized among all kinds.
Stretches upright, strong, equally favored by
Daily sun and fresh rain purely flavored.
On Appledore the stray poppy breaches
The garden's bounds and graces the lane,
A reminder, beauty belongs everywhere.
Truly then, nature's own, none to waste.

Notes from Appledore

Celia's veranda with its tangled vines
Flowering bower of private serenity
Windows cut in thick twisted greenery.

The crease of ceaseless weariness in
Her everyday routine, bouyed by the
Fine air's unsurpassed deliciousness,
Celia who heard too many words, sought
The salmon blooms of her hollyhocks
Amongst the curl of the twining hops.

Voices in the winds her company,
The calls of offshore seabirds whirling,
While nearby native St. John's Wort waves,
Gulls build scrapes amongst low grey rocks
Lay their eggs almost in the mossed paths,
The young born in these treacherous nests.

As drawn cod dries on the sun-scalded flakes
So of the children born fate prints their brows
On the wild chance-worn Isle of Appledore.

New Day

New day, new season, new star, new start
The time for celebration is here
All eyes on islands lost to time yet
Protected, improved and held dear

New solar panels embrace suns rays
Share energy, and power the place
We lessen footprints on fossil fuels
As we forge a deep friendship with space

Held as a fragment of universe
Long known to us as spirit's true home
Bless our island with gifts from above
Step by step, destined to move on

So we celebrate long stewardship
And promise to continue in kind
Our love for this rock all that matters
Connecting the earth to divine

Oceanic Hotel

The stories you could tell if the front desk could only speak,
The Pel shows you have witnessed, the many conferees
Who have roamed the dining hall and gift shops, who
Have known this Star as home, awaited place most beloved;
Love your clambered stairs, your unlocked askew rooms,
Your shared bathrooms and thin walls, your folding shutters,
Your ageless grace and ability to sway in a storm.
It all belongs within and could not otherwise be without, the Grand Hotel,
Preserved relic of past gentility, vacationers' destination,
Lives on in lore and memory, those we knew in the notebook now,
Or their ashes in the directional garden of dedicated stones.

How long can this preservation continue, forever we hope.
Oceanic, save my room for me please, I promise to return,
To set a chip of old found ceramic upon the sill,
To gather strength in my legs from your endless flights,
To throw the windows open at night, to absorb all the sounds
That layer the ocean's own rough calls while enfolded are
The gulls, the softball games by day, the shared secrets on
The porch by eve, and the vows made later in the chapel.
Oceanic, you are a vessel for generations of awakenings!
Stay with us as long as the granite can hold you in place.

Caress of the Rhinoceros

Bread and Puppet Theater is constant, listening...
Conscientious, tall on stilts, their red arrows
Swing four directions, the full arc of justice...
With decades of sustained courage they report...

The caress of the rhinoceros,
The prowess of the tiger,
The return of extinct species
And all imaginary creatures!

In an insensitive stalemate, are we 'great' yet?
You shape a solution from papier-mâché...
Prophecy, entertainment, participation,
Black lives do matter, nature is our true mother...

Give dollars for protest, not pretext.
Resist, and consist of inner strength.
We in the same boat, balance efforts
So we may continue to float.

People call for freedom, insist it realized,
Vote equality, women, environment,
Reconciliation in families, mental health,
Food for the hungry, grains of emancipation.

Inspiration and positive conspiracy
To wake spectators for further activity...
To spark involvement and sharp cultural concern,
Preserve ways to pay attention and learn.

Genius of the puppets, their making...
Kindness of the bread, its breaking...
Concern for the future, her lasting...
Design for shared peace, word casting...

Praises

High hangs the lunar pendant in the night sky
Eye that has seen all, over the ages.
It is to Her we call for our forgotten ones,
Our lost remnants, moon in heaven.....
Low drops the lunar pendant in the night sky,
Crescent to gibbous, full to waning new,
Attuned to those long-buried, within earth's folds,
Luminously smooth over the glowing stone.

The entitled enslaved us, I hear them grieve,
Remorseful now, broken, untested,
Above on the walkway, always unrested.
Grant our remains the simple peace,
Beyond all pain, all memory.

The pick, the shovel, the machines
Tore into my spirituality, beat me
To my bones again, my family,
Yet today, finally, we are born free
History with us, praises, praises be!

So unto the olden ways we haunt with word
We write for those risen, those unheard
The mysteries recovered at this hallowed site
The ghostly shapes of hovered beings by night.

Performed onsite at the ABG in October 2015.

The ghostly shape...

Photo credit: S. Flause

African Burying Ground

When in October 2003 the earth here was disturbed,
Portsmouth's African dead voices were finally heard.
This secret burying site once known as sacred ground,
Over-built by commerce but now honor-bound,
After ten-plus years of planning only just last May,
With traditional blessings, re-interred bodies in graves.

Grim as its origins, harsh as the final verdict
We call 'sankofa' and return to face the edict.
Learning our past of horrors, concerned for amends,
How to now best bless these former fellow men?
The memorial site small with a large charge on spirit,
With somber challenges that change how we see it.

Read the passages carved here, gaze at the sculpted faces.
Stroll the ribbon of pleas, solemn-scripted by enslaved.
Read the poem, the meaning, hear from captives tongues,
Sit upon the benches, ponder what must yet be done.
With wisdom from error, intent to right the past,
Let unity grow humbly, as futures are re-cast.

Recovered burying ground, prompt to peace, healing, and faith,
Lead us to a place within of beauty, truth, and grace.

Performed October 2015 as part of Blank Page Poetry with Jerome Meadows at 3S Artspace.

Rising Waters

Rising water, chance of floods,
Rains and melting snows,
Wet the print of spring this year,
Washing out the roads.
Man the sump pumps, clear the decks,
Modify your plans;
For the roots beneath the earth
Nature's gift is grand!

Peoples' lame perspectives don't
Constitute the word.
Pay attention to the clouds,
Listen to the birds.

Shell Game/Puerto Rico

We've lost everything is the cry
From islanders who've been alright
Or better up til now, our turn to
See what all this loss feels like,
The loss we have imposed in the past,
You know we have, the mother gives
And she takes, and blows away without
A look back, we strain past limits
We didn't know we had, we play
The shell game hoping to find hope
Hidden under the empty cup that
Used to hold clean water from the tap

There is no end to this story,
Its descriptions, hardships, and
The words we could write about
Waiting for basics, the trust mis-
Placed, the dotard in charge of
Our torn-to-pieces future, it is the
Satos' cry that rises in our gorge.

Slant View

Early morning Portsmouth
With the slant rays of the
Sun scattering the cast
Clouds, breaking pink
Light above the brick city,
Sloped over the tugboats.

Rounded septic trucks with
Thick flexible hoses roam
And pump the inadequate
Holding tanks at a hundred
Coffee shops. People walk,
Cars easily parked.

Soon fashionable Europeans
On their quaint historic quests
Will throng the paths.
Private scenes of Portsmouth will
Push back before daybreak
To satisfy our desire for scarcity.

Today in April, first daffodils
Accent the barren, splashes of color
In our consummate appetite for
Market Square's gentle variety,
Her ungarnished bloom and tangle.

The bridge is up every half hour,
Ships count that rise to pass,
The years have ticked off this
Tradition, water what it is
In the active Piscataqua
Its currents un-patterned.

Eyes register change and miss what
Is taken too soon, the passing of
Honor and elegance from our view,
The buildings towering on their
Humble footprints, and consciences
That can no longer sleep get rich.

Like an elderly prisoner in solitary
Confinement for a mistaken crime,
Portsmouth is still our home, she
Resonates acceptance—with a shrug,
A prayer that Strawbery Banke
Survives touristy trends.

Table Of Seasons

The faces of tiny flowers look up at me,
Their petals arranged as on a flounder,
All the important pieces to one flat side,
Their beauty that of decorative plates.
These are the pansies gifted by a friend,
Planted that dusk because I couldn't wait.

Spring, we are impatient, we pondered bulbs
Under towering snowbanks, as we endured
Grueling shoveling, and 'early warning weather.'
The sooner the annuals roots take to the soil
The better for the bounty of the pallid yard,
Waned ground-covers ride brightened tide.

We cannot have every planting we want,
But we often do receive those we need, and
We ask this spring to kindle our connections,
To resurrect intricate shapes, missed colors,
To string together garden memories like beads
Of springs we have earned from earlier years.

Soon we will traverse flagstone paths and admire
Showy blooms, soon the trees will fully leaf,
The pink buds form, flag their petals, softly fly.
These are the earliest days, magnificence still
Nuzzled at the core unfurls, gains strength,
Nourishment to sustain the incipient growth.

Rain, fair skies, when you must, the
Pattern of your fingertips on the surface
Of the giant river is like a shuttled tatted mat
All of what must be is, in its own way,
Tremulously part of a table of seasons,
And we the honored guests, our places laid.

Seasmoke Lace

Through lace curtains I can see
Sea smoke rising up from the river
Appearing as other dimensional lace,
A billowing film, filling the gap
Between New Hampshire and Maine,
A spreading band of white steam.

The kitchen quiet, even the kettle
Hums to itself, the dreaming river
With its cloud of foggy thoughts
Spills impressionism over the ledge,
The neighborhood's homes, and leaves a
Softening mist upon the angular
Cement steps and geometric brick.

Today or any day may sharpen
Like a blade, may it not?
Yet when it begins with elegance
Perhaps unfolding hours will reveal
Flowers in a shaded place imbued
With a trace of the unusual.

Weird Intimacy

There's a weird intimacy here
In my bedroom, while I half-sleep
As my mind turns over people
And events, also philosophies,
Actions and conversations, we are
All in here together, the author woman,
The black blogger, the white supremacist,
The well-meaning liberals, the students,
Promoters, volunteers, sponsors,
All in an auditorium on an unusually
Mild January day, we need to be there
As the colors of our culture are on the line.
I watch you model authentic communication
Across our different backgrounds, highlighting
Our wild misunderstandings of each other.
The seesaw has you of color higher. We
Of whiter skin weigh you down with our
Ignorance while we kick off, trying to lift.
You see us as interfering in a way that
Further diminishes your abilities. Sorrily
We only guess how to acknowledge or progress.
All our lives asleep, now you see 'whites'
Struggle to awaken as you get your feet.
The timing makes us look like clowns. But
What is our weak humiliation next to your
Four hundred years of suffering and slavery.
If we now wear labels we deserve them.
But all agreeing is not possible. The
Olive-skinned man rebels about being blamed
Lumped with the lightskins' shame.

Under his red cap he is stuffed with
A simmering rage, he seems potentially
Dangerous and un-hearing, we are repelled
While trying to comprehend, catch the current.
He steps outside and is interviewed, the man
Who disrupted the proceedings, who could have
Had a gun, who wanted confrontation, who
Made the speakers hyper-aware and cautious.
All of you are here with me while I
Recover in my bed, warm and hoping for rest.
It is intimate, steamy, swollen with
Attitudes that need to be purged, sage
And cedar, smoke and mist, tolerance
And frustration, an urge to call it quits.

Sangsara

'Handcuffed by the lord' we laughed.
The mittens sold you by the Tibetan
Were still tied together when you
Stretched them in place over cold
Fingers, 'handcuffed by the gods'
We quipped, and yes we just reviewed
The darma wheel with the shopkeeper,
She showed how the mandala revealed
Houses of sangsara well below nirvana.
All of us acknowledged our dwelling
On this ephemeral spinning planet
Where we can buy Tibetan mittens,
Twisted coils of incense, then bend
To a wet wind over Provincetown, find
Flecks of nirvana in wild coastal weather.

Showing up at Portsmouth Library for "After School Poets"

Kate consulting Dewey

Sewing haiku banner for Ceres Bakery Poetry and Art Show - April 2016

A haiku banner

"After School Poets" write their thoughts

April 1, 2016
Youth poets read at Ceres Bakery

Huxley reads original work to rapt audience in Ceres Bakery

On Star Island

Visiting museum exhibit on Star Island

Our field trip to Star Island on June 24, 2016

*Booklet with many blank pages for
drawing and writing practice*

Poems for Peace

A collection of poetry by the children of Portsmouth and beyond

Foreword for Poems For Peace

Between the springs of 2015 and 2017, as poet laureate of Portsmouth, I was afforded the opportunity to work with children in the schools, the library, the 3S art gallery, wherever we could arrange, to watch their interest in poetry blossom.

I had previously been given a similar opportunity by a close friend, who taught the life of Celia Thaxter on the Isles of Shoals in her classroom curriculum. Under her gentle guidance I gained skills to help me interact with seacoast's young people. Thank you, Ann.

Children's voices inspire in me a memory of less complicated thoughts. Anything is possible and the trust of personal power is intact. Yet all the winds of feeling blow through freely.

Some young people's poetry is included in this volume, to lift us, to demonstrate their process for our combined growth.

Poems For Peace never limits, always listens. Each poem is a call for peace which begins with inner understanding. Spend time with their poems, re-read them, go with them on their idea and word journeys.

I'm Safe

I'm in a nation that's powerful. I'm safe.
But we are peaceful.
I'm still safe.
And,
My nation has fire-power.
But it's got a heart.
I'm still safe.

- *Judah D'Antonio*

by: Eila Fitzgerald

Robin

A robin sits on my window sill singing his little song, I sit there watching him, he flaps his tiny wings he flys in a circle still singing, I watch him and feel amazed at how free this tiny bird is, he lands back on my window sill singing his little song, I sit there watching him wishing I could sing like him

- Eila Fitzgerald

Writer

Remember who will write this story.

Not the victor, but the girl with brown hair
and blue eyes and a smile
someone has finally told her is good enough.

She will write this story.
You don't have the words but
it's what she's good at.

She is the one who wakes with ink on her hands
and paper on her tongue,
and when she writes you down it will be her story
and the heartbeats you hear in the words will be hers.
Listen.
You could have loved her.
She would have let you.
Instead, you are the villain in this story,

and this is how it ends.

- *Claire Breger-Belsky*

Claire Breger-Belsky is a sophomore at Stanford University interested in literary translation, creative writing, languages, and literature. She spends most of her free time writing poetry and doing theatre. She is passionate about using theatre and other ways of storytelling to give voices to those who are rarely heard.

Jump

i was ten years old
when i jumped off the back porch feet first
into a pile of snow already muddied by my brother's eager feet

in those few fetal seconds
there was nothing but cold air
rushing everywhere
my chest opened up but i couldn't tell if I was breathing or not

then there was only snow and cold and
shock at the lack of pain

and i can't help, but wonder now
as i stand on the edge of
nothing
          and
everything
if this landing will be like the last

- *Mehli Yoder*

Terrorists Are Not True Muslims!

Killing by hand, swords and guns,
fighting to reach the highest power,
killing brothers and sons,
brothers and sons bombing and
attacking each other in the Middle East,
deaths of 200 people each day at least,
crying and crying over loved ones
while they are trying to survive,
they try so hard not to break down
wishing their loved ones would revive,
Isis, Al- Qaeda, Taliban,
they all call themselves Muslims?
They call themselves Muslims
and expect not to carry any sins?
Muslims by name but not by soul,
all they want is to gain control,
do not let them fool you,
these rumors are untrue,
do not let that feeling of hatred in your heart increase,
Islam by itself means peace,
it means peace, submission and obedience for all,
not destruction, chaos and causing a pall,
people's hatred for Islam is not decreasing,
this way, terrorist groups are winning,
trying to turn everyone against Islam is not right,
if anything, those suffering will
not go down without a fight,
take this from a young Muslim that just
wishes peace upon everyone,
it is not about who lost and who won,
terrorism is automatically associated with

"so called" Muslims who crave blood,
blood that makes the audience's eyes flood,
the people that suffer,
their chances of survival are slim
ANY TERRORIST THAT CLAIMS TO BE MUSLIM,
IS NOT A TRUE MUSLIM,
Islam is the total opposite of violence,
it is simply heaven's guidance.

- Nuha Al-Shair

Pitter Patter

Pitterpatterpitterpatter CRASH! CRASH! BANG!
An emotional storm has begun.
Pitter patter swoosh!
A friend comforts.
Pat...pat...pat
Feeling calmer.
Pat...pat.
The rain stops and the sun comes out to play in harmony.

- Huxley Schintzius

Sleep Softly

Slowly slip into slumber.
Let your body ocean calm its waves
Of rainbows and delight.
Sleep softly, my child, softly sleep.
A voice of fine silk and sharp as diamond blades sings
"sleep softly, my child, softly sleep"
Stars shine through iridescence in the abyss of night.
Sleep softly, my child, softly sleep

- Huxley Schintzius

Two weeks

Day one

I text you first
Waiting all day for your silent response,
I figure you must be exhausted from the days prior; telling off an ex and realizing
that if you won't allow yourself to have me, you don't deserve anyone
Scratch that,
Society won't allow you.

Day two

I text you again, knowing how forgetful you are
You respond bitterly, towards me or the people you just deleted from your life I am still uncertain
Whether I am included in that list I am even more uncertain of

Day three

I reread through our texts, I replay our skype conversations
I watch your eyes watch my lips through my own mind's eye
I consider the blush that is so uniquely me, that you pointed out as cute
I realize that thought now brings tears to my eyes

Day four

I have yet to bring myself to change our names on messenger
Instead I search in our conversations for key words such as 'hope' 'friends' 'break' 'kitten'
Kitten

That single word could stop my heart as it drifts off your lips
A single word
A single word that made me fall so incredibly far in love with you that if it were a gap it would go through the entire earth if it were a star it would blind us all if it were a black hole it would envelope our entire universe in one, unforgiving motion

Day five

I still have hope

Day six

Like an alcoholic, I cannot handle your withdrawal
You have become my sobriety
What happens when months have passed and I text you
And the response that lights up my screen is not a bright one of joy for the reconnection
But a final 'who is this?'

Day seven

Your name clouds my mind

Day eight

I listen to the soundtrack you made me of music you love
I cannot help but hope somehow I am closer to you through this
I beg to feel some kind of connection with you
While you on the other end have gone silent, curled into yourself

Describing that our friendship is over, it meant nothing,
Move on and forget their existence because they will forget about you

Day nine

I have come to acceptance of just friendship
The thoughts your lips have left
The jokes have grown as cold as our dormant messages

Day ten

Your name has not left my mind
The feeling of your hair has not left my fingertips
The warmth of your hug has grown cold in my breast
My hands shake as I lose my grip as I lose my mind as I lose you
And I have to face the facts that I was left alone without a thought of a goodbye
Because space is what you need and space is what you are getting

Day eleven

and I have not figured out whether I hate you or if I am just going insane
The silence kills me but you
You are dying in your own silent war that you refuse to let me in on because
you are afraid not that others will shoot me down
but that I will turn the gun on myself to escape the imprisonment of the words others have left in your mind
Words that shatter and break and tear at the person you are the person I love the
person who I know is none of these things but listens to the words still
The one who says nothing affects them
but I see through your cracks I see the bullet holes the pain the scars

the hurt the torture
I see each words of encouragement you whisper my way you have yet to find
a way to give to yourself because you are afraid
Afaid if you believe it then it will be ripped from your hands yet again
But I
I will not be ripped, torn or shattered from you
I will stay I will be your guiding light there is nothing to keep me from being there with you
Except
for your own voice

Day twelve

I have come to terms with friendship
Just as long as you will not forsake me
Will not turn around and walk out that door to leave me stranded
Not only would you be abandoning me but you would be abandoning yourself

Day thirteen

Your words of encouragement failed me today
I could not believe in myself anymore because you could not believe in me
You could not dare to reach out and show the kind of friendship we may never share again

Day fourteen

You were there
A whisper, a faint fog that I cannot handle but only look at the magnificence
of hoping, praying that it will reach me,

that it will do more than sit there
that somehow it will reach out and speak to me
And I am scared
I am scared by what runs through your mind
I am afraid that by leaving you alone I am not proving myself enough
but by texting you now you will never feel you have enough room to breath
That I will suffocate you and take your breath away
not in the romantic way, not in a fit of laughter but in good intentions hidden behind the worst actions
~
Two weeks

In two weeks you have made me lose my mind and my soul
When the day before you told me you'd talk to me tomorrow

You lied.

- Megan Todd

Dog

  A dog A dog I listin
  in my head Dogs are my
  favrit animal Dogs have chut
  ieyes they lick my face it feels
  wadery and soft I stroke
  her on her fere her fere
  is so so soft ese soft
  ese a jental rane
  on her fere.

—Hollis Ruby Cannella Matthews

    Commentary on *Dog*
    John Simon

The page on which Hollis Ruby Cannella Matthews printed the foregoing poem included as well a pair of illustrations, of a dog's face surmounted by hearts, and of a dog, so labeled, beneath a sprinkling of raindrops. The sentiment expressed by Hollis Ruby, in words and pictures, suggests a woman who will later—she is at present seven years old—visit a shelter with the purpose of offering a dog who has lost, or perhaps never had one, a home.

Young Hollis Ruby, without understanding the science, has already anticipated a shared capacity recently demonstrated, with 13 cooperative canines and an imaging machine, by Attila Andics, a neuroscientist at Eotvos Lorand University in Hungary. Reports Nell Greenfieldboyce, correspondent at the NPR Science Desk, quoting

Andics: "Dogs process both what we say and how we say it in a way which is amazingly similar to how human brains do." And the sharing of bacteria implicit in the "wadery" face licking enjoyed by Hollis Ruby, and reciprocated with the stroking of "fere" (fur), is healthful as well as enjoyable, according to a University of Colorado, Boulder study. Explains LiveScience News Editor Megan Gannon, quoting the researchers: "Recent studies link early exposure to pets to decreased prevalence of allergies, respiratory conditions and other immune disorders in later stages of development." That's some of the science of our symbiotic relationship with dogs. Hollis Ruby's poem is more concerned with fundamentals, of love and emotion, of "chut/ieyes" and a face licked by one whose fur "is so so soft ese soft/ese a jental rane." A dog that hears the words, "A dog A dog I listin/in my head Dogs are my/favrit animal," is a lucky dog, indeed. Lucky the dog who lives with Hollis Ruby.

Seven-year-old Hollis Ruby Cannella Matthews is in second grade and has brown eyes. Her mom is Wendy, her father, Brian, and her nine-year-old sister, Dewey. Hollis Ruby loves to write poems, paint, make snowmen, and play basketball. She is performing in her school variety show a song she wrote called "Just Be Yourself," self accompanied on her ukulele. She is also writing for her school newspaper an article titled, "Poems Make Your Life Better, Not Screens." Hollis Ruby loves people and dogs, especially her cousin's pug, Phoebe.

Intellectual Regression

I've always striven to be intellectually honest
But you keep telling me to remain silent
While not seeing that it's precisely this silence
That's serving as license for violence.

If we spent more time honestly debating views
Rather than being unreceptive
To anything but the dishonesty of the news
We might find error in the political correctness directive.

I'm not denying that there isn't dire need for sensitivity
But it's coming at the cost of intellectual credibility.

One side has claimed ownership of Truth
But advocating only these 'certainties'
Is corroding primary liberties
In favour of preserving delusions of inclusivity.

They've unequivocally denied direct causation
And all facets of correlation.
Alongside which we find the declaration that
They will never change their minds
(And pledge to censure those who remain unaligned).

Nothing is scarier than an individual's proclamation
Of irreversible rational castration.

Everything must be up for discussion and revision
And failure to adopt this attitude
Absolutely deserves my derision,
For without it all we speak are unsubstantiated platitudes.

Denying all dialogue
In favour of peddling a pre-emptive denunciation
Of individuals who offer justified evaluations,
Presents as an undeniably cataclysmic ligation.

Avoidance merely trumpets that something's being hidden.
And nothing's more dangerous than declaring subjects forbidden.

You claim not to understand
The large scale backlash underfoot
Supposedly unaware of your helping hand
In developing a class of the justly frustrated.

It's time for conversation
Rather than discourse repression
And this perversely pervasive dishonesty that's scaffolding
The ascension of aggression
(Which leads nowhere but international disintegration).

Our strength lies in defending our ability to question
And honestly calculate even seemingly unpalatable suggestions.

- Myla Swallow

Argue with me.

We sit and you talk,
Unaware that I balk,
As you espouse thoughts
That have been plumbed
Into the framework of your being,
Without any attempt from you towards overseeing.

Never can I question your positions,
For to you, your beliefs are decisions of discretion.

So I sit as you speak,
Withholding critique,
Because enquiry of the sort I have in mind is more criticised
Than the acquisition of your views from being socialised
Among people who are hypnotised,
To ideologies that are rarely (if ever) reviewed or revised.

When did freedom of speech
Become freedom to preach?

I don't ask for you to change your views
Only that you peruse
Other perspectives in a critical light,
To put up a considered fight when I ask you: "Why?"
It's not okay when I contradict, that you sit and decry
The heresy of my position, attempting to crucify and not clarify.

Our 'truths' are evidently not self-evident,
Meaning the absence of query should have never been etiquette.

Everyone is entitled to an opinion
Be it on traditions, villains or religions.
But the time is over for silent incredulity or public mockery.
We have more fruitful debates with children about broccoli
Then over the beliefs that govern the time we spend alive.
Respectful intellectual collision is the means to end divide.

-Myla Swallow

Homemade Candle

Wax makes candles, candles make light,
And light lights up the world.
I stand out at night with my candle so bright
with wax dripping down,
the light lights up the world.
Everybody sees it, my candle so bright.
Light going through the forest and others seeing it in the night.
Flashing through the forest, animals looking up into the darkness -
they see my light.
The trees gleaming with the reflection of my light as the animals
sleep among the branches.
All around, everything is like day - lighting up someone else's world.
Please light up my world.

- Lulu Higginson

Spring Snow

On the first day of spring
Snow fell. I don't know why.
Nothing blew. It was still.

- *Lulu Higginson*

Commentary on *Spring Snow*
John Simon

An extremely difficult task befell me in the wake of the readings by children and young adults of their poetry at Ceres Street Bakery on April 1st. I had to select one from among the poems handed to me by these young people as they departed that venerable establishment. Copies of many of those poems hang on the walls there in frames; a visit will pay dividends not only in good food and drink, but also in the opportunity to absorb the reflections of local youth on the subject of "peace." The poems explored this subject from many perspectives; I ultimately chose one that did so from that of the storied New England weather. But within Lulu Higginson's observation of a spring snowfall is so much more; in four short sentences, she records an instant of history, an energizing element of the human condition, and a fundamental aspect of science, namely, cause and effect. Winter, however thoughtfully mild this year, has chosen to persist, to resist spring's incursion, snowing on her debut and engaging in a tug-of-war with her for the temperature. Why did it snow on the first day of spring? Lulu confesses not to know. And how much more, how very much more, there is that we do not know. Anyone remember Skeeter Davis? I wasn't much older than Lulu when Ms. Davis' litany of questions in

End of the World—"Why does the sun go on shining?" "Why do the birds go on singing?" "Why does the sea rush to shore?"—emanating from one of those tabletop jukeboxes one used to find in diners, raised goose-bumps on my skinny eight- or nine-year-old arms. One comes to know by observing, and Lulu has clearly already begun to do so. "Nothing blew. It was still," she writes. The sentiment is reminiscent of the denouement of Robert Penn Warren's "Love Recognized," which concludes: "And it is not certain that the world will not be/Covered in a glitter of crystalline whiteness./Silence." How much remains stationary when the air is so. Lulu notices the stillness, the flakes accumulating into a thin white sheet laid over the shivering earth. She notices, too, that not all the questions we might ask have answers. And she sets down what happened on the first day of spring in the year 2016. Even if they have to do so through a thin veneer of snow, many things are blossoming this spring, among them a covey of young poets.

Lulu Higginson is six years old and in kindergarten. When asked why she started to write poetry, she replied: "I started because our friend Kate Leigh gave me and my sister a booklet of poems. I like poetry because I think everyone should be treated well and fairly. I like poetry because poems are nice. I like poetry because poetry is fun." Lulu participates in Portsmouth Poet Laureate Kate Leigh's "After School Poets" program, which generated many of the poems contributed to the National Poetry Month event Kate organized at Ceres Street Bakery.

I Believe

I believe everyone should have equal rights,

I believe everyone should be treated fairly,

I believe everyone should be treated with equality,

I believe everyone should treat each other with kindness,

I believe everyone should respect each other's beliefs,

I believe everyone should respect each other's words,

I believe everyone should resepct each other.

-*Ella Higginson*

My name is Ella Higginson and I wrote this poem in honor of African Americans. I got this idea when Kate Leigh came to my classroom two years ago. She taught us how to write poetry and we learned about the African Burial Ground in Portsmouth. I read this poem in honor of Martin Luther King Jr, at the Old South Church on MLK Day in 2016.

Being Female

We are told
That being a woman
Means we have a condition

That makes us weaker,
More emotional,
Easier prey

Our remedy
Is to cover up more,
Don't smile on the streets,
Don't wear shorts when you're a waitress,

And to prevent
Getting hurt,
We must take extra precaution,

I am a female,
I must learn how to break the knee of a larger man,
And how to place my hands to get out of a choke hold,
Just in case,
And hope my attacker won't be immune to pressure points.

I'm taught that the eyes are the weak point,
And to press my thumbs in their sockets,
And hope they aren't immune to pain,
So hopefully I can run away.

Being a female,
Means being taught to protect yourself against men,
While being told
"Not all men."

We are taught
To be strong like a lioness,
But act like a butterfly,
Because we can't look like we are strong,

We are taught to not walk the streets at night,
But what if I want to look at the stars?
We are taught not to go to the store without a friend,
Because strength is in numbers,
And when we're alone,
They don't care which star is in the sky,

Everything we're told
Contradicts itself.
They want me to be covered,
Tell me that my bra strap is showing,
But to be confident in my body,
Even though my body is also my weakness.

A victim is a victim.
If it mattered what we wore,
Rates would double in the summer,
But they don't.

It does not matter what we wear,
It does not matter.

The problem is the attacker:
Their minds are broken,
And all they can see is their lust.
They don't care what we wear.

Stop shifting the blame.
It's not inherently my responsibility because I'm a woman.
It's the attacker's fault,
Not the victim's.

Stop.

- Samantha Fitzpatrick

Did You Know the Dalai Lama Sometimes Swats Mosquitos?

On a balmy day in later June
He takes a breath and spares a few
That thirst for blood and wander through
His temple in Dharamsala, India
But those unlucky one or two
Annoying, yes, but thirsty too
Unfortunate to wander through
And break his concentration
Will witness in their final view
His Holy Hand descending to
In one quick motion, show them a new
And ultimate understanding of peace
More silent than the deepest meditation
They will know a true illumination
And through this fateful consecration
Never hurt again

- Mikey Ippolito

I first spoke this poem at a youth poetry event in Ceres Bakery when I was a junior at Portsmouth High School in 2016 - it was the first time I ever shared my work with a crowd of people. I wrote this piece as part of the newly formed PHS Poetry Society, with the excellent guidance and mentorship of Sherry Fawcett and Lisa McAllister. Portsmouth will always be an inextricable part of my art and my life.

Cruising

When we're gliding along the open of life
In seconds I can see a bump
And in smaller fractions of seconds
I see the wall
And I'm hit
And nothing hurts more than knowing what's going to happen,
seeing and feeling what happens, and sitting there living still
And we're going faster
We're screaming
We're laughing so hard
And then we lurch forward
And no one's angry
No one's saying anything
And when I saw that wall
All I could think was, this airbag better not deploy
Because I won't be able to see what's next the second after the wall is collided with
So this airbag better never fucking deploy
Because we're going fast
And we're screaming
And I could have sworn I just died laughing
But found myself still and alive

- Lexi Legendre

Top of Earth

If your bus ride feels any less than a cross between a boat ride and a helicopter
Maybe it's just a sad day
You look beautiful today
"Am i really" she says
And to that i say, everything always is in the morning
For a moment everything is silent
Things are still and plastered
Big oil paintings among the sky
And there's a song playing in my head
A vibrant binaural tone
And the sound of a string instrument
Chinese sung
Culture enriched
Everything always is in the morning
And for a moment your aura radiates all around you
You are the only thing i see in the entire world
You look beautiful today
Waking up
Looking at the big oil paintings among the sky
Laughing
Biting your lip
Sun spills
Cream colors

- Lexi Legendre

shame.

In the third grade, I stole my best friends necklace.
It was a silver chain,
With a shining pink pendant.
I think it came from Claire's,
Worth no more than ten dollars,
But priceless to my yearning hands.
She left for the bathroom
Leaving the object of my desire,
Lain blatantly on her desk.
I didn't think it through,
No hesitation or careful planning,
My eyes darted side to side,
And my hands reached for the prize.
I dug it deep into my pocket,
Feeling the cool of the chain lace through my fingers.
My heart skipped a beat when she walked through the door.
She showed no signs of notice,
Until she turned to me and asked.
I said I hadn't seen it, sweat forming on my brow.
The class soon turned upside down
Every child on the hunt;
For the very thing they'd never find,
Buried in the pocket of my embroidered jeans,
Scathing every inch of me.

- Amelia Sheesley

san fransisco.

We talk until words no longer hold a meaning
Laughter shatters silences in between
We walk on broken glass unseen

Reminiscing elementary days
And woodchips dug into knobby knees
Memories that burn to the tenth degree

Best of friends tied at the hip
Strings woven colorfully together
Who knew that it was always weathered

- Amelia Sheesley

cxvb.

In a world where kings rule
I wanted to be close enough to kiss your crown
But I was lower than you by miles
A peasant destined for squall and servitude
Not a glimmer of gold on my torn clothes and tattered soul
You kicked me in so many times,
and blinded by sunken eyes;
That I could not see I had a glistening crown of my own
And yours was formed from blood and bones.

- Amelia Sheesley

Sway

High in the treetops of London
There was a girl who swayed
She liked it in the treetops
She just liked it that way

- Dewey Cora Cannella Matthews

This poem was written when the poet was sitting in her favorite maple tree when she was 6 years old.

Afterword by Wendy Cannella
KATE LEIGH: MY MARY POPPINS
*Originally read at "Women Reading Women" series
at Prescott Park on August 17, 2017*

I'm here to tell you about a very special person who lives right here in Portsmouth—she is our own Mary Poppins—and I think she is practically perfect in every way—and I want to share with you one of my favorite of her poems. It's called "Strong Water."

> "Strong Water, for Edie"
>
> The strong water rolls us
> in her hands like clay.
> Though the boat cuts
> Through her skin, she
> never stops to swathe.
>
> She is of flow and matrix.
> She has all those deep,
> astonishing tricks. We
> stiffen, but she shows us
> always, how to stretch.

The poet's name is Kate Leigh, and she was our prior Portsmouth Poet Laureate, the practically perfect 10th Poet Laureate of Portsmouth. Like Poppins, Kate has educated children with wisdom, with love, with magic. She has worked tirelessly to bring poetry to young people in our schools, our coffeehouses, our art galleries, and our libraries around the seacoast area. Have you ever seen real magic happen? I have, when I watched Kate inspire a classroom of third-graders to write poems, not wanting to put their pens down after half an hour, clambering over one another to share what they had written. All this because Kate shared stories with them, stories of local 19th century poet Celia Thaxter, stories of gardening and sea air and parlors filled with paintings and pottery, stories of these many islands right off this coast, islands like the ones she writes about in her poem "Third Floor Window" where Leigh looks out and sees: Malaga, Appledore, Smuttynose, Duck. What a rich vocabulary Kate Leigh draws from these local rocks, what a rich scenery, this glorious world which closes her poem:

> All of this vision held still, [she writes] in the early daylight
> To seem a canvas, painted to remind us, how broad
> Our world, how dense our vista, how the farthest edge
> of the planet, is after all, not simply a line, but a curve.

And to prove again and again the curving of that line, Kate Leigh brought groups of young students to Portsmouth's African Burying Ground to ask questions bigger than themselves. She took groups of young students seventeen miles out to sea to visit Star Island to stretch how far they could see.

In her poem, "Salt Chop" you can see how deeply Leigh scrutinizes these crashing waves, of time, of world, of sea:

Salt Chop

> The "pop-up page" waves in our boat's wake
> Jump like marionettes on strings,
> Topped with white sliding tufts
> Of unruly forelocks. Each leaps, subsides, is
> Pulled to a peak, is dropped,
> Swirls, instantly calculates
> Infinite variety, for all time.
>
> Imagine eternity!

Yes, if you want to see magic happen, listen to Kate Leigh mesmerize a group of second-graders with the imagining of eternity, with stories of the car fire that burned Edna St. Vincent Millay's manuscript of poems to ash. And, as Kate told her hushed audience, how Millay went home and rewrote every single one of those poems, from memory and from sheer poetic will. Because do you know what Kate Leigh (a.k.a. Mary Poppins) really teaches? She teaches belief in oneself and in one's creative powers.

I know this personally because Kate ran writing workshops which my two young daughters participated in. And when my seven year old wrote a poem about chewing gum I was kind of like the mean strict controlling mother who thought well maybe you can come up with something a little better than that, but not Kate. Kate turned to my daughter and said, "That's a love poem. I think you should hold up your pack of chewing gum in your hand while you read it." I have never seen a child beam more brightly. Because what Kate Leigh gives to our young writers is not only her own strong ear for verse, or her sensitive eye for the poetic image, or her call for peace and justice, these are important, yes, but the heart of the thing, the deepest wish she grants, is the validation of our children's thoughts and hopes and strivings, their unbounded love. And that is the starting point for peace. Because Kate Leigh believes that peace is something that must be actively created. As Denise Levertov says we must work to make peace "an energy field more intense than war."

Under Kate Leigh's light touch, poets as young as six years old have given performances on stages around the city, have participated in civil rights gatherings, been published in the local newspaper, they've had poems chosen for anthologies of poems for peace, but most significantly, these seacoast children have come to believe in themselves and their powers—I'm not really talking about the power to clean up a room—but their powers of perception and expression and empathy. These children are learning, in the words of Kate Leigh, "deep, astonishing tricks," "not to stiffen, but how to stretch."

www.ingramcontent.com/pod-product-compliance
Lightning Source LLC
Chambersburg PA
CBHW041305110426
42743CB00037B/4